Beyond the Classroom:
to EOTAS

Introduction

Every week in my practice, I meet families facing what can only be described as an educational emergency.

Their child is bright, curious, sensitive—and yet, entirely unable to cope in school. Sometimes it's trauma. Sometimes it's autism. Sometimes it's chronic illness, anxiety, or a complex tangle of unmet needs. Whatever the reason, one truth becomes painfully clear: school is not working. And worse—no one seems to know what to do next.

That's where EOTAS comes in. But for too long, it has been hidden behind acronyms, misunderstood by professionals, and guarded by gatekeepers. Families are told it's "not available," "not suitable," or "not policy." Some are even coerced into home education just to get their child off a roll.

Let me be clear: EOTAS is not a favour. It is a legal right. It is the solution the law provides when traditional schooling cannot meet a child's needs. But exercising that right—asserting it confidently, understanding it fully—requires knowledge, courage, and persistence.

That's why this book matters.

Understanding EOTAS is the most comprehensive guide I've encountered for parents, educators, and professionals navigating this complex terrain. It goes beyond definitions and case law. It offers something far more powerful: clarity.

You will find legal grounding. Practical strategies. Real-life case studies. A roadmap through tribunal appeals. A vision for what inclusive education can look like outside the school gates.

And most importantly—you'll find validation. If you've ever been told your child doesn't "fit" into education, this book says: Maybe it's education that needs to change.

To every parent who has felt alone in this fight, and every professional striving to do right in a broken system—this guide is for you. Keep going. You are not wrong. You are not alone. And with the right knowledge and support, you can get the education your child deserves.

Contents Page

1. Introduction to EOTAS
2. The Legal Framework: Education Act, Section 19
3. Identifying When EOTAS is Appropriate
4. The Role of Local Authorities
5. EHC Plans and EOTAS Provisions
6. Parental Perspectives and Rights
7. Mental Health and EOTAS: Supporting Vulnerable Pupils
8. Case Studies: EOTAS in Practice
9. EOTAS vs. Elective Home Education (EHE)
10. Challenges in Delivering EOTAS
11. Innovative EOTAS Approaches and Alternative Providers
12. EOTAS and Reintegration to Mainstream
13. Personal Budgets and Funding EOTAS

14. The Voice of the Child in EOTAS Decisions

15. Accountability, Quality Assurance, and OFSTED

16. EOTAS for Pupils with SEMH Needs

17. Training, Supervision, and Multi-Agency Collaboration

18. Legal Precedents and Tribunal Outcomes

19. Future of EOTAS in a Changing Educational Landscape

20. Policy Recommendations and Best Practice Guidelines

Introduction

Education is often imagined as something that happens within the four walls of a classroom—but for thousands of children and young people in England, this is not the reality. For those with complex needs, medical conditions, trauma histories, or barriers to mainstream inclusion, the concept of "school" may not fit at all. And this is where EOTAS—Education Other Than At School—comes into play.

EOTAS is not a placement. It is a bespoke educational package arranged by the local authority when no suitable school-based provision can meet a child's needs. It is rooted in Section 61 of the Children and Families Act 2014 and Section 19 of the Education Act 1996, which impose a duty on local authorities to ensure that children who cannot attend school receive a suitable education.

Despite its potential to transform lives, EOTAS remains one of the most misunderstood, underused, and inconsistently applied areas of SEND law and practice. Parents often struggle to access it, local authorities hesitate to fund it, and professionals are unclear how to coordinate it.

This book seeks to change that.

We begin with the legal foundations before moving through practical steps, real case studies, and professional reflections. We explore everything from tribunal outcomes to creative, flexible delivery models—including forest schools, one-to-one tuition, therapeutic input, and online learning. Most importantly, we keep the child's needs and aspirations at the heart of every chapter.

Whether you are a parent battling for an appropriate education, a SENCO overwhelmed by EHC plan amendments, or a policymaker designing inclusive pathways—this book will provide clarity, courage, and community.

Chapter 1: Introduction to EOTAS (Education Other Than At School)

What is EOTAS?

Education Other Than At School (EOTAS) is a provision made by a local authority for children who, for a variety of complex and legitimate reasons, cannot attend a mainstream or special school. It is not home education by choice (EHE), but a duty-bound solution under law to ensure a child's right to education is upheld.

Key Characteristics of EOTAS:

- Commissioned by the Local Authority
- Tailored to the child's needs
- Often supported by an Education, Health and Care Plan (EHCP)
- Can include a mix of tuition, therapy, vocational learning, and digital access
- Delivered in the home, community, specialist centres, or virtually

Why EOTAS Exists:
EOTAS serves children who:

- Have severe anxiety or trauma responses
- Have been permanently excluded or emotionally based school non-attenders (EBSN)
- Suffer with medical conditions that make school attendance impractical
- Are awaiting a suitable placement and cannot attend a current school

The Law Behind EOTAS:

1. Section 19 of the Education Act 1996 requires the local authority to arrange suitable education at home or elsewhere if a child of compulsory school age is unable to attend school due to illness, exclusion, or other reasons.

2. Section 61 of the Children and Families Act 2014 allows local authorities to arrange special educational provision outside of school when it would be

inappropriate for that provision to be made in a school setting.

What EOTAS Is Not:

- A loophole to avoid school attendance
- A placement type (like a PRU or AP)
- Elective Home Education (EHE)

The Rising Need for EOTAS:
With increased diagnoses of autism, mental health needs, and the impact of post-pandemic school refusal, EOTAS has become an essential route for many families. However, the landscape is patchy and inconsistent across England—leading to postcode lotteries and legal battles.

Myths and Misconceptions:

- *"EOTAS means you have to teach your child yourself."*
  ➤ No. The LA must commission professionals.
- *"You can't get EOTAS unless all schools have failed."*

➤ No. If school is inappropriate for the child, EOTAS is an option.

- *"Only children with EHCPs can get EOTAS."*

    ➤ While EHCPs are common, Section 19 also applies to children without one.

Chapter 2: The Legal Framework — Understanding the Law Behind EOTAS

Education Other Than At School (EOTAS) isn't just a helpful concept—it is embedded in statutory law. Understanding the legal framework is essential for anyone navigating the EOTAS process, whether you are a parent, practitioner, or policymaker. This chapter explores the key pieces of legislation, guidance, and case law that underpin EOTAS provision in England.

🏛 1. Section 19 of the Education Act 1996

This is the cornerstone of alternative provision. It states:

"Each local authority shall make arrangements for the provision of suitable education at school or otherwise than at school for those children of compulsory school age who, by reason of illness, exclusion or otherwise, may not for any period receive suitable education unless such arrangements are made for them."

Key points:

- It applies to all children of compulsory school age, not just those with EHC Plans.
- It mandates education that is full-time (or equivalent) and "suitable" to the child's age, ability, aptitude, and any special educational needs.
- The local authority cannot wait indefinitely or provide part-time hours unless explicitly justified by the child's needs.

This section is often cited in legal challenges when a child is left without education, especially after exclusions or during long periods of waiting for a placement.

---

2. Section 61 of the Children and Families Act 2014

This provision applies specifically to children and young people with Education, Health and

Care Plans (EHCPs). It gives local authorities the power to:

"Arrange for any special educational provision to be made otherwise than in a school or post-16 institution or a place at which relevant early years education is provided."

When does this apply?

- When it would be inappropriate for the child to receive the special educational provision in a school setting.
- This might be due to extreme anxiety, trauma, medical fragility, or other barriers.

Crucially, the law says the inappropriateness must relate to the child, not to what provision is available in the area or what is convenient for the authority.

📌 3. SEND Code of Practice (2015)

While not law, the SEND Code of Practice is statutory guidance under the Children and

Families Act 2014. It gives clarity on expectations for EOTAS arrangements. Paragraphs particularly relevant include:

- Paragraph 10.30:

"Where a child or young person has an EHC plan, the local authority must secure the special educational provision specified in the plan. This may include provision arranged otherwise than in a school."

- Paragraph 10.61:

"The child's parent or the young person may request that some or all of the special educational provision in an EHC plan be delivered otherwise than in a school."

These passages reinforce that parental request, if backed by evidence, must be considered seriously.

---

4. Judicial Precedents: What the Courts Have Said

There have been several legal cases shaping how EOTAS is interpreted. Here are key examples:

- NN v Cheshire East (2016):
  The tribunal found that even where there are theoretical placements available, if a school setting is inappropriate for the child, then EOTAS must be considered.

- Derbyshire County Council v EM (2019):
  The judge ruled that the local authority had unlawfully delayed in arranging provision under Section 19.

- R (T) v London Borough of Wandsworth (2022):
  This case clarified that LAs must fund and coordinate suitable provision, not leave families to organise it themselves.

These rulings reinforce that suitability is child-specific, not based on resources or local convenience.

---

5. How the Law Applies in Practice

Situation	Legal Responsibility	Typical Outcome
Child is too anxious to attend school	Section 19	LA must arrange suitable full-time education, possibly EOTAS
EHCP specifies EOTAS	Section 61	LA must deliver that provision in full
Parent requests EOTAS during tribunal	Section 61 + CoP 10.61	Tribunal may order EOTAS if school is found inappropriate
School placement breaks down with no alternative	Section 19	Interim EOTAS or tuition required immediately

⚠️ 6. Common Legal Pitfalls by Local Authorities

- Refusing to consider EOTAS unless "all schools fail"
- Offering part-time hours as a default
- Delaying action while "awaiting placement"
- Denying funding or therapeutic support in EOTAS packages
- Treating Section 61 as a last resort, rather than a viable option

All of these can be challenged through judicial review or tribunal, and many have been overturned due to failure to meet statutory duties.

✅ 7. Legal Checklist for Families and Professionals

If you're advocating for EOTAS, use this legal checklist:

- ☑ Has the child been without suitable education for more than 15 days?
- ☑ Is the child medically or emotionally unable to attend school?
- ☑ Does the EHCP say school is inappropriate, or can that be evidenced?
- ☑ Has the LA responded to your written request under Section 61?
- ☑ Are you documenting delays and correspondence?

---

8. Template Legal Wording for Requests

"In accordance with Section 61 of the Children and Families Act 2014, I request that my child's EHC Plan is amended to specify that special educational provision be made otherwise than in a school, due to the inappropriateness of a school setting for meeting their needs. This is supported by [insert evidence]."

And for children without EHCPs:

"Under Section 19 of the Education Act 1996, the local authority has a duty to arrange suitable education for my child, who is currently unable to attend school due to [reason]. I request urgent confirmation of what provision is being made."

---

9. Summary

EOTAS is legally robust, though poorly understood. Section 19 provides universal protection, while Section 61 provides specialist support through EHCPs. These duties are non-negotiable, time-sensitive, and child-centered.

Knowing the law—and asserting it when necessary—is the first step to securing an education that works.

Chapter 3: Identifying When EOTAS Is Appropriate

While the legal framework for EOTAS is clear, deciding when it is appropriate to request or implement Education Other Than At School can be complex. This chapter explores the key indicators, scenarios, and evidence that suggest EOTAS may be the right solution for a child or young person.

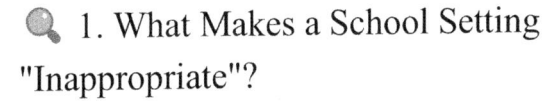

🔍 1. What Makes a School Setting "Inappropriate"?

The law does not require all schools to fail before EOTAS can be considered. Instead, it focuses on whether education in a school setting is inappropriate for the child's individual needs. Common reasons include:

- Severe school-based anxiety or trauma
- Medical fragility or immunocompromised conditions

- Sensory processing difficulties that are exacerbated by school environments
- Extreme social communication needs (e.g. autistic children overwhelmed by noise, crowds, or unpredictability)
- A history of repeated exclusions, school-based distress, or placement breakdowns
- Complex neurodivergence or PDA (Pathological Demand Avoidance)

These issues often mean that the very nature of school—bells, uniforms, timetables, transitions—is not tolerable or safe for the child.

⚠️ 2. Red Flags That EOTAS Might Be Needed

Red Flag	Why It Matters
Frequent school refusal despite support	May indicate underlying anxiety or trauma

Red Flag	Why It Matters
CAMHS or paediatric recommendation to remain home	Shows medical necessity
Child has been out of school for over 15 days	LA's duty under Section 19 triggered
Existing EHCP is not being delivered	May warrant EOTAS under Section 61
EHCP review says school is not meeting need	Opens route for formal EOTAS consideration
Therapeutic needs cannot be met in school	EOTAS can incorporate therapy as core provision

Tip: These indicators should be documented. Keep medical notes, professional reports, daily logs, and school communication.

3. Professional Evidence That Supports EOTAS

To strengthen a request for EOTAS, it helps to gather the following:

- Letters or reports from CAMHS, psychologists, psychiatrists, or GPs stating school is inappropriate
- SENCO and school reports acknowledging distress or unsafe behaviours
- Evidence of past exclusions, incidents, or unmet need
- EHCP reviews and annual reviews where concerns have been raised
- Tribunal rulings in similar cases (for comparison)

The stronger and more specific the evidence, the more likely an LA or tribunal will accept that EOTAS is required.

👪 4. The Role of Parents and the Child's Voice

Parents often identify the need for EOTAS before professionals do, as they witness the deterioration in their child's wellbeing daily.

Key signs parents might observe:

- Panic attacks before school
- Regression in toileting, eating, or sleep
- Withdrawal, shutdowns, or meltdowns
- Self-harming or suicidal ideation
- Improved wellbeing on non-school days

Equally important is the voice of the child or young person. Even very young children can describe how school makes them feel—fearful, sick, overwhelmed, unsafe. The Code of Practice places a legal emphasis on this voice being heard.

🧠 5. Differentiating EOTAS from Temporary Non-Attendance

Sometimes children are off school temporarily due to illness or a placement gap. This does not always mean EOTAS is appropriate long term.

Situation	Likely Outcome
Child is temporarily unwell	Section 19 tuition until recovery
Child has been excluded	Section 19 AP or tuition
Child is recovering from trauma	Interim plan, may transition back to school
Child has long-term needs making school inappropriate	Formal EOTAS package under EHCP likely needed

---

6. When Schools Acknowledge the Need

Some schools will proactively support the identification of EOTAS—particularly where the school setting is clearly not working. Others may resist due to budgetary or reputational concerns.

Good practice looks like:

- Honest conversations at Annual Reviews
- Schools gathering evidence of unmet need
- Collaboration with parents and external professionals

Poor practice looks like:

- Blaming parenting
- Threatening fines or prosecution
- Minimising the child's distress
- Avoiding Annual Reviews to delay EOTAS discussion

---

7. The Pre-EOTAS Checklist

Use this tool to assess readiness for requesting EOTAS:

✅ Question

- ☐ Has the child missed more than 15 days of school?
- ☐ Do professionals believe a school setting is inappropriate?
- ☐ Is the child showing signs of distress linked to school attendance?
- ☐ Has the EHCP been reviewed and deemed unsuitable in school?
- ☐ Is there documented evidence (reports, emails, logs) to support this?
- ☐ Has the child's voice been considered in EHCP reviews or reports?

If you've checked 4 or more boxes, EOTAS is likely to be a suitable option.

---

8. Real-Life Scenarios

Amira, Age 12 — Autistic with Selective Mutism

After trying three mainstream schools and one special school, Amira became entirely non-verbal and began self-harming. Her family obtained CAMHS support and an educational psychologist's report stating school was "actively harmful." EOTAS was granted with home-based learning, speech therapy, and nature-based education.

Liam, Age 14 — SEMH and Trauma

Liam had been excluded five times and placed in an alternative provision that did not meet his therapeutic needs. His behaviour deteriorated. A tribunal ruled that a tailored EOTAS plan including clinical therapy, mentoring, and outdoor learning was required.

---

9. Summary: When to Pursue EOTAS

EOTAS should be considered not as a last resort, but as the first appropriate step when:

- The child's needs cannot be met in school

- Attendance causes harm
- There is multi-agency support for a different educational model
- The child has stopped making academic or emotional progress

When the system isn't working, it's not the child who should adapt—it's the system that must.

Chapter 4: The Role of Local Authorities in EOTAS

Local Authorities (LAs) in England have legal duties and practical responsibilities when it comes to Education Other Than At School (EOTAS). Understanding what LAs must do—and what they cannot lawfully avoid—empowers families and professionals to advocate for appropriate education and challenge systemic failures.

This chapter explores how LAs are supposed to assess, arrange, and fund EOTAS packages and how to respond when they do not.

🏛 1. Legal Duties of the Local Authority

Local Authorities have two core duties in relation to EOTAS:

- Under Section 19 of the Education Act 1996:

They must provide a suitable education for children of compulsory school age who are unable to attend school for reasons such as illness, exclusion, or "otherwise."

- Under Section 61 of the Children and Families Act 2014:

They can arrange special educational provision otherwise than in a school, if it would be inappropriate for the provision to be made in a school.

Key takeaway: These duties are not optional. They are legally binding and enforceable via judicial review or tribunal.

---

2. The EOTAS Decision-Making Process

In theory, the process is simple. In practice, it's often delayed, misunderstood, or resisted.

Step-by-step outline:

1. Identification of Need
   – Child unable to attend school
   – Professionals support out-of-school education

2. Evidence Gathering
   – Medical or psychological reports
   – School logs and EHCP reviews

3. Parental or Professional Request
   – Letter/email to LA requesting EOTAS (under Section 61 or 19)

4. LA Assessment
   – May commission an Educational Psychologist or medical advisor
   – May consult the EHCP team or consider alternative schools

5. Decision and Drafting
   – EOTAS provision outlined in Section F of the EHCP
   – Named provision (tuition, therapy, setting, etc.)

6. Funding and Commissioning
   – LA arranges and funds the provision directly or via providers

7. Monitoring and Review
   – Provision reviewed at least annually under the EHCP

3. What Local Authorities *Should* Do

Task	Expected Action
Acknowledge formal request	Respond within 20 working days
Consult professionals	Commission updated advice if needed
Review EHCP	Hold review meeting or tribunal
Involve the child and family	Seek input in the planning process
Specify and quantify provision	Clearly detail the what, who, when, and how in Section F
Monitor delivery	Ensure commissioned services are being delivered as agreed

Task	Expected Action
Review annually	Use Annual Review to evaluate impact and adapt

4. What Local Authorities Must NOT Do

Unlawful Practice	Explanation
Delay EOTAS decisions indefinitely	Duty under Section 19 is immediate
Refuse to consider EOTAS unless all schools have failed	Law requires focus on appropriateness, not availability
Offer "educational" babysitting or token tuition	Education must be suitable, full-time or equivalent
Place burden on parents to find provision	LA must arrange and fund, not delegate to families

Unlawful Practice	Explanation
Undermine EHCP by vaguely defining Section F	Provision must be detailed, specific, and legally enforceable
Use lack of funding as an excuse	Resource constraints do not override legal obligations

5. When Things Go Wrong: Common Failures

- Inadequate or missing provision for months at a time
- "Ghost" EHCPs with no named provider, tutor, or therapist
- Local Authorities claiming EOTAS is "not available"
- EOTAS offered with unlawful conditions (e.g. parents must teach)

- Delays in funding, leaving children without any input

---

6. Remedies and Legal Recourse

When a Local Authority fails in its duty:

1. Complaint to the Local Authority

Begin with a formal complaint outlining the failure and referencing legal obligations.

2. Judicial Review

Used when there's an urgent or serious breach (e.g. child with no education). Judicial review can force LAs to act quickly.

3. SENDIST Tribunal

If EOTAS is refused or omitted from an EHCP, parents can appeal to tribunal to secure it under Section 61.

4. Local Government Ombudsman

This route may secure compensation and recommendations after a service failure, especially where delays caused harm.

💰 7. Funding EOTAS: What LAs Must Cover

Local Authorities are responsible for funding:

- Tuition (online or in-person)
- Specialist therapeutic input (e.g. SALT, OT, psychotherapy)
- Equipment and learning materials
- Travel to and from any approved EOTAS location
- Supervision and safeguarding where appropriate
- Technology (e.g. laptops for online learning)

Funding must not be based on "what's cheapest"—it must be based on what is suitable.

---

8. Building a Collaborative Relationship

While many families must advocate assertively, collaboration can yield faster results. Encourage your LA to:

- Listen to the voice of the child
- Work transparently
- Consider creative solutions (e.g. blended tuition, mentoring)
- Partner with trusted local providers
- Offer trial EOTAS programmes with review points

---

9. Summary

Local Authorities are central to the success—or failure—of EOTAS. They have strict legal duties and must not let budget, staffing, or prejudice delay action. When operating lawfully and ethically, LAs can help shape innovative, life-changing educational packages for the children who need them most.

Chapter 5: EHC Plans and EOTAS Provisions

For children and young people with special educational needs and disabilities (SEND), an Education, Health and Care Plan (EHCP) is a legally binding document that specifies their support. When school is inappropriate for a child's needs, an EHCP can be used to formally secure EOTAS under Section 61 of the Children and Families Act 2014.

This chapter focuses on how EOTAS provision is captured, funded, and enforced through the EHCP.

---

1. The Legal Framework: Section 61 Revisited

As outlined in earlier chapters:

"A local authority may arrange for any special educational provision... to be made otherwise than in a school... if satisfied that it would be inappropriate for the provision to be made in a school or post-16 institution."

To trigger Section 61 EOTAS:

- The child must have an EHCP
- There must be evidence that a school setting is inappropriate for the provision
- The child's needs must be central—not convenience, availability, or cost

---

2. What EOTAS Should Look Like in an EHCP

An effective EOTAS package will be clearly specified in Section F of the EHCP, which covers *special educational provision*. Here's what it should include:

Provision	Example
Teaching	1:1 home tuition for maths and English, 10 hours per week
Therapy	Weekly SALT and OT sessions

Provision	Example
Mentoring	Weekly therapeutic mentor in the community
Vocational learning	Digital skills course through local college
Resources	Specialist reading software and tablet
Timetable	Structured plan covering 25 hours/week equivalent
Location	Provision delivered in home/community/local centre
Monitoring	Half-termly reviews by SEND caseworker and provider

All EOTAS provision must be detailed, specific, and quantified—just like provision in any EHCP.

---

3. Drafting Strong EOTAS Sections in an EHCP

Use clear, enforceable language in Section F. For example:

❌ Vague:

"Child will receive some online tutoring."

✅ Specific:

"Child will receive 5 hours per week of 1:1 online maths tuition from a qualified SEND tutor provided by [provider], delivered via Zoom."

Avoid phrases like:

- "As appropriate"
- "Access to"
- "May benefit from"

These are legally weak and unenforceable.

---

4. Section I of the EHCP – The Named Placement

For EOTAS to be legally formalised, Section I must name 'EOTAS' rather than a school or college.

✏️ Example:

"Education Other Than At School (EOTAS) as per Section 61 of the Children and Families Act 2014."

Sometimes it may say:

"Provision will be made otherwise than in a school."

This means the Local Authority accepts that no setting is appropriate and provision will be arranged entirely outside a school environment.

💬 5. Who Can Request EOTAS in an EHCP?

- Parents
- The young person (post-16)
- Schools (rarely, but can support)
- Educational Psychologists or CAMHS

- Tribunal panel (SENDIST)

Requests are typically made:

- During an Annual Review
- As part of an EHCP Needs Assessment
- As a response to failure of placement
- During a SENDIST appeal

---

6. What Happens During an EOTAS Tribunal Appeal

If the Local Authority refuses to include EOTAS in an EHCP, you can appeal. The SEND Tribunal will look at:

- Whether a school placement is "inappropriate" for the child
- Whether EOTAS is more suitable and effective
- Medical or professional evidence
- The child's views

- Attempts to support school placement

The tribunal can order the EHCP to name EOTAS in Sections F and I, along with a full specification of the support.

---

7. Funding EOTAS via EHCPs

EHCPs enable access to:

- Top-up funding (Element 3)
- Personal budgets (optional, not essential)
- Direct payments (where agreed)

EOTAS can be funded:

- Through direct commissioning by the LA
- Via parents or carers using a personal budget (if agreed and suitable)
- Through third-party providers delivering on behalf of the LA

Important: LAs cannot deny EOTAS on the basis of cost alone if the provision is the only appropriate option.

8. Case Law Example: EOTAS Ordered via EHCP

Case: P v East London LA (2021)
A young person with autism, PTSD, and severe anxiety was unable to access school despite multiple placement attempts. CAMHS reports confirmed school was "clinically unsafe." Tribunal outcome: EOTAS package including tuition, psychotherapy, and forest school activities. The LA was ordered to specify all provision in Section F and name "Education Otherwise" in Section I.

9. Summary

When school is inappropriate, the EHCP is a powerful legal tool to secure high-quality, out-of-school provision. Section 61 of the Children and Families Act 2014 allows for EOTAS to be written into the plan—provided the child's needs justify it.

A robust EOTAS EHCP must:

- Be evidence-based
- Include detailed, enforceable provision in Section F
- Name "EOTAS" in Section I
- Be regularly reviewed for impact and progress

Chapter 6: Parental Perspectives and Rights

Parents are often the driving force behind successful EOTAS arrangements. They are the ones who see their children's distress firsthand, who notice when school no longer works, and who push against the system to get their child the support they need.

This chapter explores the rights, responsibilities, and lived experiences of parents navigating EOTAS.

👪 1. Parents as Advocates

In many cases, EOTAS only becomes a reality because a parent refuses to accept that their child's suffering is acceptable. Parents are often forced to:

- Gather evidence
- Submit requests
- Challenge LA decisions
- File appeals to SENDIST

- Coordinate provision themselves while waiting

This unpaid, emotionally exhausting labour is a form of advocacy. Without it, many children would remain without education.

---

2. Your Legal Rights as a Parent

Parents have several statutory rights in relation to EOTAS:

Right	Legal Basis
To request EOTAS	Children and Families Act 2014, s.61
To contribute to EHCP reviews	SEND Code of Practice 9.168
To appeal to tribunal	SEN and Disability Regulations 2014
To request a personal budget	Children and Families Act 2014, s.49

Right	Legal Basis
To be involved in decision-making	Article 12 of the UNCRC & CoP Chapter 9

You do not need to be an expert in the law—but understanding your basic rights can help you hold professionals to account.

🗣 3. Common Parental Experiences

Frustration:

"They kept insisting school could meet her needs, even though she was in meltdown every morning."

Exhaustion:

"I felt like I was the one doing all the educating and therapy while the LA ignored us."

Relief:

"Once we got EOTAS, he finally started learning again. He smiled for the first time in months."

Empowerment:

"Now I trust my instincts. I know what my child needs, and I know my rights."

---

4. Tips for Parents Seeking EOTAS

- Document everything: Keep emails, medical notes, school records
- Request in writing: Always follow up phone calls with written requests
- Reference the law: Mention Section 61 or Section 19
- Get professionals on board: Ask your GP, CAMHS, or EP for support
- Don't wait for a crisis: You can request EOTAS early if needed
- Prepare for a fight: EOTAS often requires resilience and formality

---

5. When Parents Are Told "No"

Local Authorities may say:

- "We don't do EOTAS."
- "It's not available in our area."
- "We need to try another school first."

These responses are unlawful if they disregard the evidence that school is inappropriate. You have the right to:

- Submit a formal complaint
- Escalate to judicial review
- Appeal to SENDIST

---

6. Supporting Other Parents

Parents who have navigated EOTAS often become informal support networks for others. Join:

- Facebook groups (e.g. Not Fine In School)
- Local SEND support forums
- National organisations (e.g. IPSEA, SOS!SEN)

You are not alone—and your story may help another family.

✳ 7. Summary

Parents are not obstacles to be managed—they are partners in education. EOTAS success stories often begin with a parent who said, "This isn't right. We need something different." You have legal rights, a critical voice, and the power to help your child thrive.

Chapter 7: Mental Health and EOTAS – Supporting Vulnerable Pupils

A significant proportion of children and young people receiving EOTAS do so due to mental health difficulties. Whether it's anxiety, trauma, or co-occurring neurodivergence, school can become a source of harm rather than growth.

This chapter explores the intersection of mental health and education, and how EOTAS can provide healing, stabilisation, and learning.

---

1. Mental Health Conditions Common in EOTAS Cases

- Severe anxiety or generalised anxiety disorder (GAD)
- Post-Traumatic Stress Disorder (PTSD)
- Depression
- Emotionally Based School Avoidance (EBSA)
- Eating disorders

- OCD or intrusive thoughts
- Self-harming behaviours
- Suicidal ideation

These are not signs of weakness or defiance. They are real, clinical issues that can make traditional schooling intolerable.

🏫 2. When School Becomes a Trigger

In some cases, school environments:

- Trigger panic attacks or shutdowns
- Reinforce feelings of failure or trauma
- Lack sensory-safe spaces
- Have rigid expectations that clash with the child's emotional state

These children may stop sleeping, eating, or speaking. For them, attending school is not "challenging"—it is dangerous.

---

3. The Legal Duty Still Applies

Even if a child has mental health issues, the right to education remains. LAs must:

- Recognise school-based anxiety as a legitimate barrier
- Avoid forcing children back into harmful placements
- Commission education in a therapeutic, adapted manner
- Work with CAMHS, paediatricians, and families to co-design support

Section 19 and Section 61 still apply.

---

4. Role of CAMHS and Mental Health Professionals

CAMHS can:

- Diagnose and validate anxiety, PTSD, and depression
- Recommend time out of school or EOTAS

- Provide supporting letters for tribunal
- Offer in-home or virtual therapy sessions

A CAMHS report stating "school is inappropriate" is often decisive in securing EOTAS.

🛠 5. Therapeutic Provision in EOTAS

EOTAS can be more than just tutoring. For children with mental health needs, provision may include:

- Weekly psychotherapy or counselling
- Nature-based therapy or forest school
- Art, music, or play therapy
- Equine therapy
- Somatic/body-based trauma recovery
- Mentoring with trauma-informed staff

The goal is to heal, stabilise, and reconnect the child to learning.

6. Voice of the Child in Mental Health Cases

Children with anxiety often:

- Know exactly what they need
- Feel unheard or disbelieved
- Are frightened of returning to school

Give them space to express:

- What causes their anxiety
- What makes them feel safe
- What they want from learning

Include these views in EHCPs and Annual Reviews.

---

7. Outcomes: What the Research Says

Studies show:

- Children in EOTAS often experience reduced anxiety and improved wellbeing

- Re-engagement in education becomes possible when emotional safety is prioritised
- Attendance rates improve when education is flexible and person-centred

---

8. Summary

EOTAS is not an escape from education—it is a pathway back to it, for children whose mental health makes school unsafe. With the right therapeutic provision, vulnerable pupils can heal, grow, and succeed in environments built around their emotional needs.

Chapter 8: Case Studies – EOTAS in Practice

While law and policy are crucial, nothing illustrates the power of EOTAS better than real stories. This chapter shares anonymised, representative case studies that show EOTAS in action—and the difference it can make.

Case Study 1: Rosie, Age 10 – Autistic with Severe Anxiety

Background: Rosie experienced daily panic attacks at school. Her attendance dropped to 14%. She became non-verbal and developed gastrointestinal symptoms linked to stress.

Provision:

- 1:1 home tuition (12 hours per week)
- Weekly OT and art therapy
- Fortnightly mentor for social skills
- Monthly educational psychology input

Outcome: After 6 months, Rosie began writing again and asked to join an online group class. She now receives 20 hours/week education and is thriving.

📖 Case Study 2: Amaan, Age 14 – PTSD After Exclusion

Background: Amaan was permanently excluded following a behavioural incident in Year 8. He witnessed a violent assault outside of school and developed PTSD. AP placements failed.

Provision:

- 10 hours/week online tutoring
- Weekly trauma-focused CBT
- Gym membership and personal mentoring
- Digital music production course

Outcome: Amaan is working toward GCSEs, sleeping better, and wants to pursue sound engineering.

Case Study 3: Maya, Age 6 – Rare Medical Condition

Background: Maya's immune system disorder made it unsafe to attend school during winter months. Her EHCP named EOTAS.

Provision:

- 8 hours/week home tuition
- Virtual group sessions with peers
- Specialist SALT input remotely
- Termly hospital school check-ins

Outcome: Maya is making steady academic progress, remains medically stable, and feels socially connected.

Chapter 9: EOTAS vs. Elective Home Education (EHE)

Understanding the Differences, Overlaps, and Legal Implications

Parents and professionals often confuse EOTAS (Education Otherwise Than At School) with Elective Home Education (EHE). While both involve learning outside of a traditional school setting, they are entirely different in law, funding, purpose, and process.

This chapter breaks down the differences, helps you identify the right pathway, and addresses the risks of misclassification by local authorities.

⚖ 1. Key Differences: EOTAS vs. EHE

Feature	EOTAS	Elective Home Education (EHE)
Legal basis	Section 61 CFA 2014 / Section 19 EA 1996	Section 7 of the Education Act 1996
Who arranges it?	Local Authority	Parents
Who funds it?	Local Authority	Parents
EHCP required?	Usually, but not always	Optional
Professional involvement	Yes – tuition, therapy, specialists	Only if arranged privately
Is it a parental choice?	No – it's for when school is inappropriate	Yes – voluntary choice to home educate

Feature	EOTAS	Elective Home Education (EHE)
Tribunal accessible?	Yes – EOTAS can be ordered by tribunal	No – EHE cannot be ordered by tribunal

2. What is Elective Home Education (EHE)?

EHE is a parental choice to educate a child outside of school. It may be chosen for philosophical, cultural, religious, or dissatisfaction-based reasons.

- No funding is provided
- No EHCP required
- No entitlement to LA support (though some choose to engage)
- The responsibility for education lies solely with the parent

It is not a legal alternative when school is unsuitable due to need—that's what EOTAS is for.

---

3. When EHE is Inappropriately Suggested

Some Local Authorities:

- Pressure parents to "electively" home educate instead of offering EOTAS
- Present EHE as a "quicker" or "easier" option
- Mislead parents into deregistering their child without explaining the consequences

Important:
Once a child is removed from school under EHE, the LA no longer has a duty to arrange education under Section 19. This can delay or derail access to EOTAS or EHCP reviews.

---

4. What the Law Says

Under Section 7 of the Education Act 1996, parents are required to:

"…cause [the child] to receive efficient full-time education suitable to their age, ability and aptitude, and to any special educational needs they may have, either by regular attendance at school or otherwise."

EHE is lawful, but only when:

- It is truly voluntary
- It is not coerced
- The parent fully understands their responsibilities

---

5. When EOTAS is More Appropriate than EHE

Choose EOTAS if:

- Your child is unable to attend school for medical or psychological reasons

- Professionals recommend alternative provision
- Your child has an EHCP that requires delivery outside school
- You want the LA to remain responsible for arranging and funding provision

---

6. Parent Voices: Real-World Confusion

"They said if I de-registered, it would be quicker to sort things out. We didn't know we were giving up his right to education."
— *Liam's mum, Manchester*

"I thought I had to choose between homeschooling or nothing. No one told me about EOTAS until a charity helped."
— *Jasmine's dad, Kent*

---

7. What to Ask Your LA Before Accepting EHE

Before signing any EHE form or letter, ask:

- Are you offering EOTAS under Section 61 or Section 19?
- Will you continue to fund any education or therapy?
- Is this truly a voluntary decision or are there other options?
- If I deregister, what legal duties does the LA still have?

If in doubt, do not deregister until you receive proper legal advice or advocacy support.

---

8. Tools to Distinguish and Decide

Scenario	Appropriate Option
You want to teach your child at home for religious or personal reasons	EHE
Child has PTSD and cannot tolerate any school setting	EOTAS

Scenario	Appropriate Option
You can afford private tutors and want autonomy	EHE
Your child has an EHCP and needs specialist therapy	EOTAS
LA says they have no school place and offers nothing else	EOTAS (Section 19 duty applies)

---

9. Summary

EOTAS and EHE both involve learning outside school, but they are not interchangeable.

EOTAS is a statutory duty, arranged and funded by the Local Authority for children whose needs cannot be met in school.

EHE is a parental choice, where the responsibility—and the cost—rests entirely with the family.

Always seek independent advice if you're unsure which is being offered.

Chapter 10: Challenges in Delivering EOTAS

Barriers, Pitfalls, and What Can Be Done About Them

While EOTAS offers a powerful solution for children whose needs cannot be met in school, its delivery is often fraught with challenges. These range from bureaucratic delay to inconsistent funding, and from professional misunderstandings to deep-rooted prejudice against alternative education.

This chapter explores the systemic, logistical, and cultural barriers to successful EOTAS implementation—and offers strategies for overcoming them.

---

1. The Challenge of Gatekeeping and Delay

Many families report facing:

- Months of silence or delay after requesting EOTAS

- Repeated school placement attempts, despite evidence of unsuitability
- Denials based on "policy" rather than law

This is known as gatekeeping—when LAs intentionally or unintentionally create hurdles that delay or prevent access to lawful provision.

Why it happens:

- Lack of training among LA staff
- A fear of "opening the floodgates"
- Financial concerns
- Poor understanding of legal thresholds

---

2. Budget Constraints and Resource Refusal

EOTAS is often incorrectly perceived as "too expensive." In reality, many EOTAS packages cost less than full-time specialist school placements.

Still, LAs may:

- Offer reduced hours to save money

- Refuse therapy or specialist input
- Push for part-time AP or tuition only

⚠ *Important: Cost alone cannot lawfully justify refusal of appropriate provision.*

✖ 3. Poorly Written EHCPs

One major challenge is the vagueness of EOTAS sections within EHCPs. Common issues include:

- No mention of EOTAS in Section I
- Use of non-specific language ("access to", "may benefit from")
- Lack of quantified provision (no hours, frequency, or provider details)

The result: parents cannot enforce the provision, and children go without.

🏚 4. Lack of Suitable Tutors or Therapists

Even when EOTAS is agreed, LAs may struggle to:

- Source qualified 1:1 tutors
- Commission consistent therapeutic input
- Arrange safe, consistent delivery

This is often due to:

- Underinvestment in alternative provision markets
- Limited relationships with non-school providers
- High demand and poor planning

---

5. Fragmentation and Lack of Monitoring

Without a school setting, EOTAS provision can become disconnected, with no single person overseeing delivery, quality, or progress. Risks include:

- Poor safeguarding and data-sharing
- Inconsistent attendance or engagement

- No academic tracking or outcome measurement

A high-quality EOTAS package must include:

- Named lead professional
- Coordinated reviews
- Regular communication between tutors, therapists, family, and LA

---

6. Professional Misunderstanding and Bias

Many professionals still misunderstand what EOTAS is—or view it as inferior. Some believe:

- "Children need to be in school to learn."
- "Parents are just avoiding responsibility."
- "EOTAS is too lenient."

This stigma can influence:

- Annual Review outcomes
- Referrals and assessments
- Decisions about transition or reintegration

Overcoming this requires training and culture change.

---

7. Isolation and Mental Health Risks for Families

When provision is inconsistent or absent, parents report:

- Becoming de facto teachers, carers, therapists
- Severe stress, burnout, and relationship strain
- Financial hardship due to lost earnings
- Social isolation for both child and family

EOTAS done badly becomes EHE by default—without consent or support.

---

8. Tribunal as a Last Resort

While many families win EOTAS at SENDIST, the process is:

- Long (3–8 months)
- Stressful
- Resource-intensive
- Legally complex

Families without representation may struggle to:

- Present sufficient evidence
- Understand relevant legal arguments
- Sustain the process emotionally and financially

---

9. What Can Be Done

Challenge	Strategy
Gatekeeping	Quote law (s.19 & s.61), make formal complaints, escalate to ombudsman
Funding refusals	Demand costed alternatives, gather comparable EOTAS costs

Challenge	Strategy
Poor EHCPs	Submit formal request to amend Section F and I
Provision gaps	Request provider panel or sourcing support
No coordination	Ask for named EOTAS caseworker and monthly meetings
Tribunal barriers	Seek free legal support (IPSEA, SOS!SEN, SOSSEN, SENDIASS)

10. Signs of a Well-Delivered EOTAS Package

- ✅ All provision is detailed and quantified in EHCP
- ✅ Child has full-time or equivalent education hours
- ✅ Professionals are named and accountable

- ✅ Education and therapy are integrated
- ✅ Family has support, not just expectations
- ✅ Progress is regularly reviewed and evidenced
- ✅ Child is happy, engaged, and thriving

✳ 11. Summary

EOTAS is only as effective as its delivery. The barriers—financial, systemic, legal, cultural—are real, but none are insurmountable. With the right legal awareness, advocacy, and accountability, families and professionals can demand the EOTAS provision that children not only need—but are *entitled* to by law.

Chapter 11: Innovative EOTAS Approaches and Alternative Providers

Rethinking What Education Can Look Like Outside the School Gates

Education Other Than At School (EOTAS) does not mean "less than" or "second best." When done well, EOTAS can be creative, individualised, and deeply transformative. This chapter showcases innovative approaches and diverse providers that make EOTAS flexible, meaningful, and effective.

🌱 1. The Power of Personalised Learning

EOTAS thrives when:

- Provision is co-designed with the child and family
- Interests and strengths are central
- Education is shaped around wellbeing, not forced conformity

Flexible, child-centred models unlock learning by removing pressure and meeting pupils where they are.

---

2. Nature-Based Learning and Forest Schools

For children with sensory processing difficulties, anxiety, or trauma, the outdoors provides:

- Calm, regulation-friendly environments
- Hands-on, movement-based learning
- Opportunities for confidence-building and connection

Forest schools, bushcraft programmes, and outdoor learning mentors are increasingly used in EOTAS to re-engage pupils through real-world exploration.

---

3. Online and Virtual Learning Platforms

For tech-savvy or housebound pupils, online platforms can offer:

- National Curriculum-aligned lessons
- Live tutor interaction
- Flexible schedules
- Exam preparation support

Providers include:

- Academus Online
- MyTutor
- InterHigh
- Learnopolis
- LA-commissioned Zoom/Teams sessions with local tutors

Digital access must be accompanied by regular feedback, SEN differentiation, and offline breaks.

---

4. Creative and Therapeutic Education

For children who have disengaged from traditional learning, creative provision can reignite curiosity:

- Music and songwriting sessions
- Digital animation and film editing
- Photography and art therapy
- Drama and movement workshops

When education is integrated with therapy, outcomes improve across emotional, social, and academic domains.

🤝 5. Community and Charity-Led Provision

Many EOTAS packages benefit from partnerships with:

- Local youth organisations
- Equine therapy centres
- Farms, allotments, and conservation projects
- Boxing clubs and martial arts instructors

- Faith-based or cultural education networks

These providers often fill the relational gap left by school disengagement.

---

6. Case Study: Blended EOTAS for a Year 9 Learner

Luca, 13, SEMH and PDA diagnosis

Day	Provision
Monday	2 hours 1:1 maths tuition at home
Tuesday	Forest school session (3 hours)
Wednesday	Virtual English & science lessons
Thursday	Art therapy and mentoring
Friday	Gym session with personal mentor

Total: 25 hours/week. All provision reviewed monthly by a SEND caseworker and child.

---

7. LA-Approved and Independent Tutors

Some Local Authorities maintain an EOTAS provider framework—a pre-approved list of tutors, therapists, and mentors. Others outsource to national education services.

Key considerations:

- Are they qualified in SEND?
- Are they DBS-checked?
- Are outcomes monitored?
- Do they work trauma-informed?

Parents can request specific tutors or propose new providers, subject to LA approval.

🌐 8. Building a Holistic Package

The best EOTAS isn't just academic—it meets:

- Educational needs
- Therapeutic needs
- Social needs
- Vocational or life-skills needs

This might mean combining:

- 1:1 English and maths
- OT sessions
- Cooking, budgeting, and transport training
- Youth mentoring
- Work experience or volunteering

9. Summary

EOTAS opens the door to education that is diverse, meaningful, and dignified. With the right creative thinking, alternative providers can help children heal, grow, and succeed far beyond what any classroom alone could achieve.

Chapter 12: EOTAS and Reintegration to Mainstream

Can You Go Back—and Should You?

For some children, EOTAS is a permanent solution. For others, it can be a bridge to future reintegration. This chapter explores when and how children might return to mainstream (or specialist) settings—and when they shouldn't.

---

1. When Reintegration Might Be Appropriate

Reintegration can be considered if:

- The child expresses interest
- Mental health has stabilised
- Needs have changed or been met
- A new, more appropriate school becomes available

The process must be:

- Child-led

- Flexible
- Gradual
- Reversible

🚫 2. When Reintegration is Inappropriate or Harmful

Reintegration should not occur when:

- It is based on LA funding concerns
- The child remains in crisis or unwell
- A suitable school place still doesn't exist
- The child strongly opposes it

For some, the school system isn't fit for their needs. EOTAS may remain the most humane and effective solution.

🪜 3. Steps Toward Reintegration (When Appropriate)

Step	Description
1. Trial visits	Short, supported exposure
2. Taster days	Attend specific lessons only
3. Reduced timetable	Slow build-up of hours
4. Shadowing	Peer mentoring or buddy system
5. Dual provision	Blended timetable across settings
6. Full transition	Only if sustained success occurs

Every step must be reviewed, optional, and tailored.

💬 4. The Child's Voice in the Process

The most important question is:

"Do you feel ready—and do you want to?"

Their answer should shape the entire process. Children should be:

- Involved in planning
- Able to express doubts or fears
- Offered alternatives if reintegration fails

---

5. Professional Support for Reintegration

Reintegration is most successful when supported by:

- A named keyworker
- Educational psychologist
- CAMHS/mental health practitioner
- SENDCo or reintegration officer
- Trusted adult or mentor

These professionals should coordinate regular multi-agency reviews.

---

6. School Responsibilities During Reintegration

If a child is returning to a school, that setting must:

- Receive transition funding if needed
- Put a robust SEND support plan in place
- Offer emotional support and curriculum flexibility
- Involve parents and carers closely

---

7. What Happens If It Fails?

Reintegration failure is not a child's fault. If distress reappears, the child can return to:

- A revised EOTAS package
- Specialist setting (if suitable)
- Dual-rolled arrangements

Plans should include an "exit strategy" to avoid trauma.

8. Summary

Reintegration may work for some—but only if it serves the child's best interests. The aim isn't to "fix" the child so they can cope in school. It's to provide the education that works best for *them*, whether that's back in class, out in the woods, or learning from home with a laptop and a sketchpad.

Chapter 13: Personal Budgets and Funding EOTAS

Who Pays, How It Works, and What Parents Need to Know

Funding is one of the most misunderstood—and misrepresented—aspects of EOTAS. This chapter explains how Local Authorities pay for EOTAS, what personal budgets are, and how parents can ensure their child gets what they're entitled to.

---

1. Who Is Responsible for Funding EOTAS?

If EOTAS is:

- Ordered by tribunal
- Named in Section I of the EHCP
- Supported by Section 19 for children without EHCPs

Then the Local Authority must pay for all provision required.

This includes:

- Tuition
- Therapy
- Equipment
- Software
- Travel (if applicable)
- Any agreed support

---

2. What is a Personal Budget?

A personal budget is an optional mechanism that allows families to have input into how EOTAS funding is spent.

There are three types:

1. Notional budget: LA holds and commissions services
2. Direct payment: Money given to family to arrange provision

3. Third-party budget: Managed by another provider on the family's behalf

Families do not need to accept a personal budget to access EOTAS.

---

3. Applying for a Personal Budget

To request a personal budget:

- The child must have an EHCP
- You must identify which parts of Section F you'd like to manage
- The LA must agree it will:
    - Achieve good outcomes
    - Be cost-effective
    - Be deliverable with accountability

The LA cannot unreasonably refuse—but they *can* decline direct payments if safeguarding or financial issues arise.

---

4. What Can the EOTAS Budget Be Used For?

Approved Use	Common Examples
Tuition	Tutors, online lessons, 1:1 teaching
Therapies	OT, SALT, psychotherapy, art therapy
Resources	Laptops, software, sensory tools
Activities	Outdoor learning, vocational courses
Travel	Taxi fares for EOTAS visits
Admin	Keyworker costs, service coordination

All spending must match the needs identified in the EHCP.

---

5. What It Cannot Be Used For

- School uniforms
- Unrelated recreational trips
- Non-educational childcare
- Private school fees (unless named in Section I)

Spending must be monitored with regular receipts and reporting.

---

6. Common Issues with EOTAS Funding

- LAs offering only minimal hours (e.g. 5–10/week)
- Refusing therapy costs
- Delaying payment or reimbursements
- Capping budgets arbitrarily
- Forcing parents into personal budgets they don't want

Tip: Reference the EHCP and tribunal outcomes to hold LAs to account. The child's needs—not cost-saving—must guide funding.

---

7. Summary

Funding is a legal responsibility, not a negotiation. If EOTAS is required, the LA must pay for everything the child needs to receive a suitable education. Personal budgets can provide flexibility—but are not mandatory, and no family should be pressured into taking on what is the LA's job.

Chapter 14: The Voice of the Child in EOTAS Decisions

Listening, Valuing, and Acting on What Matters Most

At the heart of every EOTAS decision is a child or young person with thoughts, feelings, fears, hopes—and rights. Too often, their voices are overlooked in favour of what adults believe is "best." This chapter examines the legal, ethical, and practical importance of involving children meaningfully in EOTAS.

👶 1. The Legal Framework

The law is clear: children have a right to be heard in decisions that affect them.

Legal Right	Source
Right to express views freely	Article 12, UN Convention on the Rights of the Child
Right to participate in EHCP processes	Children and Families Act 2014
SEND Code of Practice	Paragraphs 1.6, 9.2, and 9.22 emphasise child participation

Children must be involved in EHCP reviews, tribunal processes, and planning EOTAS—regardless of age or communication style.

🗣 2. Why the Child's Voice Matters in EOTAS

Children know:

- What makes them feel safe
- What causes distress
- What environments help or hinder learning
- What their goals, dreams, and limits are

Involving them:

- Improves decision quality
- Builds trust
- Increases engagement in education
- Reduces trauma from forced transitions

---

3. How to Capture the Child's Views

Method	Suitable for
Face-to-face discussion	Verbal, neurotypical children

Method	Suitable for
Drawing and art-based expression	Younger or selectively mute children
"All About Me" templates	All ages, particularly those with SEND
Video or voice notes	Children who prefer asynchronous communication
Trusted adult or advocate support	Children with anxiety or trauma
Symbol-based communication tools	Non-verbal or AAC users

Important: Involvement must be genuine, ongoing, and non-tokenistic.

---

4. What Children Say About EOTAS

"I feel like I can breathe when I learn at home."
— *Kieran, 11, with PDA*

"I don't get shouted at anymore. I actually like learning now."
— *Sophie, 13, with autism*

"Being outside helps my brain think straight."
— *Zac, 14, in forest school EOTAS*

"Please don't make me go back. I'm still scared."
— *Anonymous, 10, after trauma-based school refusal*

---

5. Involving the Child in EHCP Reviews

Best practice includes:

- Preparing the child beforehand
- Letting them attend part or all of the meeting
- Using visuals, checklists, or sentence starters
- Including a written "child's views" section in the plan

- Recording how their views influenced decisions

---

6. Advocacy and the Right to Be Represented

Children and young people (especially 16+) may:

- Appoint their own advocate
- Be represented at tribunal
- Make their own request for EOTAS (if over 16)

SENDIASS and advocacy charities can provide direct support.

---

7. Summary

Children aren't passive recipients of education—they are the people education is for. EOTAS succeeds when it is designed *with* the learner, not just *around* them. The most important question we can ask is:

"What would *you* like your education to look like?"

Chapter 15: Accountability, Quality Assurance, and OFSTED

Who's Watching the Watchers in EOTAS?

With no physical school to monitor, who ensures that EOTAS provision is effective, safe, and lawful? This chapter explores accountability structures, the role of OFSTED, and how Local Authorities can (and must) quality-assure non-school education.

---

1. Who Is Responsible for Monitoring EOTAS?

Stakeholder	Responsibility
Local Authority	Primary duty to monitor, review, and evaluate provision
EHCP Case Officer	Should review delivery and outcomes termly

Stakeholder	Responsibility
Tutors/Therapists	Must submit progress reports
Parents/Carers	Report on engagement, effectiveness, concerns
OFSTED	Inspects LA SEND provision overall—not individual EOTAS setups

🛠 2. What Should Be Monitored in EOTAS?

- Attendance (realistic and flexible tracking)
- Curriculum coverage or progression
- Engagement and wellbeing
- Impact of therapeutic input
- Achievement of EHCP outcomes
- Safeguarding and lone working protocols

Note: Monitoring must be trauma-informed, not punitive.

3. What Should a Good Quality Assurance System Include?

- A named coordinator for the child's package
- A calendar of reviews (at least every term)
- Written reports from all providers
- Evidence of progress toward EHCP outcomes
- Family and child feedback
- Safeguarding checks and DBS compliance
- Contingency plans for illness or provider breakdown

4. OFSTED and EOTAS

OFSTED does not inspect individual EOTAS tutors or home provision. However, it:

- Reviews LA performance in SEND Area Inspections
- Evaluates AP/EOTAS strategies
- Checks how EHCP outcomes are being met

In inspections, weak EOTAS arrangements are often flagged as:

- "Lack of oversight"
- "Inconsistent provision"
- "Failure to meet Section 19 duties"

---

5. Red Flags in EOTAS Provision

- No timetable or schedule
- Tutors with no SEND experience or qualifications
- Vague or no recording of academic/therapeutic progress
- No line of accountability

- Provision stops for weeks without explanation

If these occur, families should raise concerns immediately—first with the LA, then with the ombudsman or tribunal if unresolved.

---

6. What 'Good' Looks Like

- ✅ Clear EHCP
- ✅ Provision is specific, consistent, and suitable
- ✅ Regular reviews by a caseworker
- ✅ DBS-checked professionals
- ✅ Progress recorded and shared
- ✅ Issues resolved quickly
- ✅ Child is learning and thriving

---

7. Summary

EOTAS does not mean "off-grid." Every hour delivered, every therapist involved, and every learning outcome promised must be monitored, reviewed, and improved. Local Authorities are accountable—and families have the right to demand transparency, quality, and child-centred care.

Chapter 16: EOTAS for Pupils with SEMH Needs

Understanding and Supporting Social, Emotional, and Mental Health Learners

SEMH (Social, Emotional and Mental Health) is one of the most common categories of need for which EOTAS is sought—and one of the most misunderstood. This chapter explores the intersection between SEMH and education, and how EOTAS can be adapted to support these learners.

---

1. What Does SEMH Mean?

SEMH refers to emotional or behavioural difficulties that impact a child's ability to learn and engage. It includes:

- Anxiety and trauma
- Attachment disorders
- Depression
- Self-harm

- Risk-taking behaviour
- Withdrawal, shutdown, or aggression

It often co-occurs with:

- Autism
- ADHD
- PTSD
- Family instability
- School trauma

---

2. Why School Can Fail SEMH Learners

School environments often:

- Are too rigid, loud, or overstimulating
- Prioritise compliance over relationship
- Use punitive behaviour policies (detention, isolation, exclusion)
- Lack trauma-informed practice

This can lead to:

- Frequent exclusions or "managed moves"
- School refusal or EBSA
- Escalating crisis

---

3. What EOTAS Offers SEMH Learners

A good EOTAS package for SEMH:

- Centres relational safety
- Offers consistency and predictability
- Prioritises emotional regulation over grades
- Includes therapeutic support

Examples:

- Daily mentoring with a key adult
- Trauma-informed tuition (low pressure, high nurture)
- Nature-based regulation work
- Weekly psychotherapy or CBT

- Unstructured creative time with reflective dialogue

🔄 4. Flexibility is Key

SEMH learners need:

- Flexible timetables and pacing
- The ability to pause and reset
- Calm spaces and sensory adaptations
- Consistent adults (minimal staff turnover)

EOTAS should allow for dynamic, week-by-week adjustments as the child's mental health evolves.

🧘 5. Therapeutic Approaches That Work

Approach	Suitable For
CBT	Anxiety, self-esteem, reframing thoughts

Approach	Suitable For
Play Therapy	Younger children, trauma recovery
Art/Music Therapy	Expression through creativity
Somatic Therapy	Body-based trauma release
EMDR	Complex PTSD
Nurture Mentoring	Daily relationship-based regulation

6. Safeguarding in SEMH EOTAS

Some SEMH learners may be:

- In care or on a CIN/CP plan
- At risk of exploitation or self-harm
- Without trusted adults outside EOTAS

Safeguarding systems must:

- Be robust, multi-agency, and trauma-informed
- Include regular welfare checks
- Involve consent and agency wherever possible

---

7. What Progress Looks Like in SEMH EOTAS

Progress isn't always linear or academic.

It might mean:

- Reduced shutdowns or outbursts
- Improved sleep and eating
- Building relationships again
- Attending every session for a week
- Starting to talk about feelings

All of this matters—and should be celebrated and recorded.

---

8. Summary

SEMH learners need more than grades—they need healing, consistency, and care. EOTAS can provide that in ways the school system often cannot. When shaped around regulation, relationship, and rhythm, EOTAS gives SEMH children a chance to not just survive—but truly thrive.

Chapter 17: Training, Supervision, and Multi-Agency Collaboration

Empowering Professionals to Deliver High-Quality EOTAS

A strong EOTAS package requires more than funding and legal compliance. It depends on skilled, supported professionals working together around the child. This chapter focuses on the essential role of training, supervision, and joined-up working in sustaining safe, effective provision.

---

1. Who Delivers EOTAS?

Common professionals include:

- 1:1 tutors (academic or therapeutic)
- Occupational therapists (OT)
- Speech and language therapists (SALT)
- Clinical or counselling psychologists
- Art, music, or play therapists

- Keyworkers or mentors
- Caseworkers and EHCP coordinators

Each plays a vital part—but must not work in isolation.

---

2. Training Requirements for EOTAS Providers

All providers must have:

- Enhanced DBS checks
- Safeguarding training (updated regularly)
- Knowledge of SEND Code of Practice
- Trauma-informed practice understanding
- Skills in flexible and relational approaches

Desirable extras:

- PDA awareness
- De-escalation training (e.g. PRICE or Team Teach)

- Neurodiversity-affirming teaching strategies
- Mental health first aid

🐾 3. Clinical Supervision and Reflective Practice

Professionals working with high-need pupils (especially those with trauma, SEMH, or safeguarding concerns) must access supervision. This allows them to:

- Reflect on emotional impact
- Share strategies
- Avoid burnout
- Improve practice

Supervision is especially crucial for:

- Therapists
- Mentors
- Keyworkers

- Lone-working tutors

🤝 4. Multi-Agency Collaboration: Why It Matters

In EOTAS, no school gate or staff room connects the team. So collaboration must be intentional.

Essential partners:

- Parent/carer
- Tutor(s)
- Therapist(s)
- SEND caseworker
- CAMHS or paediatrician
- Social worker (if applicable)

Tools that support collaboration:

- Shared communication logs
- Regular review meetings
- Co-authored EHCP review documents

- Secure online platforms for updates

---

5. Summary

Professional skills, reflective space, and team communication are the invisible infrastructure behind successful EOTAS. When providers are trained, supported, and connected, children thrive—and the burden on families is reduced.

Chapter 18: Legal Precedents and Tribunal Outcomes

Case Law That Shaped the EOTAS Landscape

Understanding how EOTAS decisions are made in law helps professionals and families make stronger arguments. This chapter outlines key SEND tribunal decisions and judicial reviews that clarify EOTAS rights.

---

1. Why Legal Precedents Matter

Tribunal and judicial review outcomes:

- Clarify the meaning of "inappropriate"
- Highlight unlawful LA behaviour
- Set useful examples for future cases
- Empower parents to assert their rights

---

2. Notable Tribunal Cases

NN v Cheshire East (2016)

The tribunal found that school was inappropriate due to anxiety, even though places were available.
→ Established that availability doesn't equal appropriateness.

M v Lancashire (2019)

A child with PTSD was repeatedly excluded. The tribunal ordered EOTAS with trauma-informed therapy and tuition.
→ Confirmed that emotional harm justifies EOTAS.

QK v Hackney (2021)

An autistic child with extreme sensory needs could not tolerate school settings. Tribunal required fully home-based provision.
→ Upheld EOTAS as a primary—not fallback—option.

---

3. Judicial Review Cases

R (T) v Wandsworth (2022)

LA failed to arrange education while debating placement. The High Court ruled this breached Section 19.

→ LAs must act immediately when school is not accessible.

R (W) v Birmingham (2020)

Refusal to offer EOTAS due to "lack of funding" was found unlawful.

→ Budget is not a valid reason to deny EOTAS.

---

4. Lessons from the Case Law

- EOTAS must be considered when *school is inappropriate*, not just when all options are exhausted.

- Mental health and sensory processing issues can make school unsuitable.

- LAs must act promptly to deliver education when a child is out of school.

- Vague EHCP wording and delay are grounds for legal challenge.

5. Summary

Case law affirms what families and professionals often know instinctively: that the right education is the one that works. When LAs fail to act, tribunals and courts uphold children's rights—and order the EOTAS they need.

Chapter 19: The Future of EOTAS in a Changing Educational Landscape

Reimagining Education for the 21st Century Learner

EOTAS is growing—not because children are failing, but because the system is failing them. As more families turn to alternative provision, we must ask: what should the future look like? This chapter explores trends, innovation, and policy developments shaping the next generation of EOTAS.

---

1. The Rise in Demand

Drivers of increased EOTAS demand include:

- Rising anxiety, EBSA, and school trauma
- Post-pandemic disengagement
- Inflexible mainstream curriculum
- Neurodivergence awareness
- Broken SEND systems

More families are saying, "My child cannot thrive in school as it is."

---

2. Technological Shifts

EOTAS is increasingly powered by:

- Virtual classrooms and adaptive platforms
- AI-based learning tools
- Online exam access
- Teletherapy and remote mentoring

But access and digital poverty remain challenges.

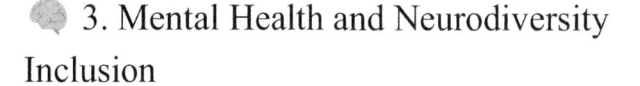

---

3. Mental Health and Neurodiversity Inclusion

New models must prioritise:

- Therapeutic learning spaces
- Sensory-friendly environments
- Trauma-informed practice

- Co-production with neurodivergent pupils

Neurodiversity-affirming pedagogy is the future—not compliance-based models.

🏛 4. Policy Recommendations for Reform

1. Make EOTAS more visible in national SEND policy
2. Create EOTAS provider accreditation schemes
3. Allow flexible timetabling as standard
4. Fund LA EOTAS officers and teams
5. Ensure OFSTED accountability for EOTAS quality
6. Protect families from LA pressure to deregister

🔺 5. Innovations Emerging in the Sector

- Therapeutic micro-schools

- Blended learning hubs
- Parent-led cooperative learning spaces
- EOTAS mentoring networks
- Virtual group learning pods

The future of education is plural, flexible, and child-led.

---

6. Summary

EOTAS is not a last resort—it's a vision of what education could be: relational, personalised, and empowering. The future lies in reimagining education as something we build *around* the child, not something they must fit into.

Chapter 20: Policy Recommendations and Best Practice Guidelines

Building a Better EOTAS System for All

After hundreds of pages of law, case studies, and lived experience, one truth stands clear: EOTAS works when it is planned, funded, and delivered with care. This chapter distils the book's key lessons into concrete policy and practice guidance for Local Authorities, educators, providers, and national leaders.

---

1. National Policy Recommendations

- Add EOTAS to official DfE SEND training for local authorities and schools
- Create a national EOTAS register for tracking and research
- Protect families from coerced elective home education
- Ensure equitable funding parity with specialist placements

- Include EOTAS inspection frameworks in OFSTED evaluations

---

2. Best Practice for Local Authorities

- Appoint named EOTAS case officers
- Develop local EOTAS provider panels
- Create a family-friendly request process
- Offer trial packages where full provision is delayed
- Ensure full compliance with EHCP law and Section 19 duties

---

3. Best Practice for Providers

- Deliver trauma-informed, SEN-aware tuition
- Submit regular reports and progress updates

- Collaborate with family and other professionals
- Attend reviews and EHCP meetings
- Prioritise relationship and emotional safety

---

4. Best Practice for Families

- Keep written records of all communication
- Be proactive in gathering evidence
- Know your legal rights—and quote them
- Involve the child meaningfully at every stage
- Ask for support early—and seek advocacy if needed

---

5. Tools to Measure Success

Success in EOTAS should be judged by:

- Child's wellbeing and engagement
- Achievement of EHCP outcomes
- Family satisfaction
- Reduction in school-based trauma
- Progress in communication, self-regulation, and life skills

---

6. Summary

A thriving EOTAS system is built on trust, creativity, legal literacy, and compassion. When done right, it offers not just education—but healing, hope, and a future for those who might otherwise be left behind.

Printed in Dunstable, United Kingdom